CRYSTA
UNICOR

2022

CRYSTAL UNICORNS 2022
A LAUGHING LOBSTER BOOK 978-1-913906-74-0
Published in Great Britain by Laughing Lobster an imprint of Centum Publishing Ltd.
This edition published 2021.
1 3 5 7 9 10 8 6 4 2

Illustrations by Charlotte Archer.

Laughing Lobster an imprint of Centum Publishing Ltd, 20 Devon Square, Newton Abbot, Devon, TQ12 2HR, UK
9/10 Fenian St, Dublin 2, D02 RX24 Ireland

books@centumpublishingltd.co.uk

LAUGHING LOBSTER AN IMPRINT OF CENTUM PUBLISHING LIMITED. Reg. No. 08497203

A CIP catalogue record for this book is available from the British Library.

Printed in China.

MEET THE UNICORNS

Discover lots of fun facts about Crystal Unicorn and her friends.

CRYSTAL UNICORN

LIVES IN: Crystal Castle

LIKES: crystals, gems, jewels and flying

Can you give Crystal Unicorn a makeover by transforming her colours so she looks different?

GEM AND JEWEL UNICORN (TWINS)

LIVE IN: Crystal Castle

LIKE: playing games, puzzles and ice cream

DAISY UNICORN

LIVES IN: Crystal Castle

LIKES: flowers, woods and exploring

Go Exploring

Follow the clues below to work out which friends are exploring where. When you find their location, write their initials on the map.

Find Rainbow Unicorn.

- Go north 4 squares.
- Head west 1 square.
- Drop south 2 squares.

Spot Crystal Unicorn.

- Head east 2 squares.
- Go north 5 squares.
- Turn west 1 square.

Where is Filbert Frog?

- Move north 2 squares.
- Go east 2 squares.
- Head north 2 squares.

Race to it and track Moonbeam Unicorn.

- Head north 6 squares.
- Turn east 2 squares.
- Go south 3 squares.

Find Loveheart Unicorn!

- Head north 4 squares.
- Go east 1 square.
- Move south 3 squares.

Now write some instructions to explain how to find Sparkle Unicorn.

N
W
E
S
START

Rainbow Spotter

Can you spot 10 differences between the pictures below?

RAINBOW WATERFALL

Add every colour of the rainbow to the picture below.

Unicorn Creations

Trace over the lines and add some colour to finish off the unicorn friends.

Hello Team Unicorn

Discover what makes each of these friendly unicorns unique.

Shimmer Unicorn

LIVES IN: Unicorn Castle

LIKES: parties, cupcakes, presents and balloons

Moonbeam Unicorn

LIVES IN: Unicorn Castle

LIKES: daydreaming, a full moon and sleeping

SPARKLE UNICORN

LIVES IN: Unicorn Castle
LIKES: her friends, cupcakes and flying

RAINBOW UNICORN

LIVES IN: Unicorn Castle
LIKES: rainbows, fashion accessories and grooming her mane

Can you spot 10 mini rainbows on the page?

Jigsaw Jumble

Can you work out which pieces go where to complete the picture of the unicorn meadow?

INTO THE WOODS

Colour by numbers and follow the colour key to transform these unicorns.

MATCH UP!

Can you help Gem and Jewel draw lines between these objects to match them into pairs?

Say Hi to the Unicorns

These sparkly, shimmery unicorns love to dance and prance with their friends.

Stardust Unicorn

LIVES IN: Crystal Castle

LIKES: stars, flying, crystals and exploring

Loveheart Unicorn

LIVES IN: Crystal Castle

LIKES: climbing, flying, swimming and exploring

STARLIGHT UNICORN

LIVES IN: Unicorn Castle

LIKES: shooting stars, midnight feasts and dancing

Can you match the tiaras into pairs?

BFF

Everything is better with friends by your side! Who's your BFF?

Draw or stick in pictures of you and your best friend in the frames below, and then fill in the BFF bio.

My BFF's name is

They are _____ years old

We have been BFFs since

Their favourite food is

Their favourite hobby is

Fill in this page with your bestie.

My fave thing about my BFF is

My BFF's favourite thing about me is

Our fave thing to do together is

We are different because

We are the same because

We will be friends forever and always because

ME		MY BFF
	KITTENS OR PUPPIES?	
	CUPCAKES OR SWEETS?	
	CHOCOLATE OR CRISPS?	
	DANCING OR SINGING?	
	READING OR SPORT?	
	ART OR CRAFTS?	
	SNOW OR SUNSHINE?	
	TV OR MOVIES?	

Where Am I?

Can you help Gem work out where Jewel is playing, using her clues?

A

Rainbow Waterfall

B

Over the Rainbow

C

Crystal Caves

1 Oooh, I'm chilly, it's cold here but the sky looks magical.

2 There are lots and lots of tall trees and the grass has turned purple.

3 Everything is light and sparkly here, even though I am inside.

D

UNICORN WOODS

F

CRYSTAL CASTLE

E

UNICORN CASTLE

6

There is so much space here to gallop and afterwards I'm off to the castle for cake.

5

Wee-heeeee! I am flying high above a rainbow in lots of fluffy clouds.

4

Splish splash... I love to chill out here. It's so cool and the noise of the flowing water is wonderful.

Hide & Seek

Can you spot 10 unicorns hiding in the woods?

SAY HI TO THE UNICORN FRIENDS

Discover lots of fun facts about these friendly animals.

Did you know that butterflies can taste with their feet?

LILI LADYBIRD

LIVES IN: the enchanted forest

LIKES: tap dancing, singing and somersaults

Ladybirds can have spots, stripes or no markings at all.

FLUTTERSHY BUTTERFLY

LIVES IN: the enchanted forest

LIKES: flowers, flying and playing games

CHIRPY CHICK

LIVES IN: the enchanted forest

LIKES: chatting, stories and visiting her friends for tea parties

BILL BUTTERFLY

LIVES IN: the enchanted forest

LIKES: flying, flowers, trees and nectar

HARRIET HORSE

LIVES IN: the enchanted forest

LIKES: sparkly gems and jewels, prancing and her unicorn friends

HA HA!

What do stylish frogs wear?

Jumpsuits.

Croooooak!

FILBERT FROG

LIVES IN: the enchanted pond

LIKES: jumping, swimming and poking his tongue out

Add some colours to these ladybirds so each one looks different.

CAN YOU KEEP A SECRET?

Take the quiz and discover how good you are at keeping secrets.

1 How do you feel when a friend shares a secret with you?

- (A) I feel glad that they trust me and will promise to keep it a secret.
- (B) A bit worried, but will do my best to keep their secret safe.
- (C) I don't want to know. I hate being asked to keep secrets.

2 When a friend tells you a secret, you ...

- (A) Say nothing. Secrets are always safe with me.
- (B) I might tell my mum or another bestie, but only if they ask.
- (C) Tell lots of people, I am hopeless at keeping things to myself.

3 You're with your BFF when they have a really embarrassing moment. What do you do?

- (A) Keep it between us, that's what friends are for.
- (B) If it was really funny I might tell someone else, but make them promise not to share.
- (C) I'd just have to share it with our other BFFs, too.

4 A friend wants to share someone else's secret. What do you do?

- (A) Tell them to stop. I don't want to hear secrets I'm not supposed to know.
- (B) Let them tell me, as it might help them to share.
- (C) Listen carefully. Everyone likes a bit of gossip.

MOSTLY A'S

You are a true super-hero secret keeper. Your friends know their secrets are always safe with you. You know the importance of keeping quiet and keeping secrets. But you also know that it is okay to tell a secret to a parent or grown-up if you think a friend might be hurt or in trouble.

MOSTLY B'S

You do really try to keep people's secrets but sometimes you just can't help letting them slip. Don't worry, this still makes you a good friend but try to do as your friends ask when they share their secrets and they will return the favour when you share yours with them.

MOSTLY C'S

You love to talk and have a gossip which means that secret keeping is not your best skill. It's okay to let your friends know if you find it hard to keep secrets under wraps. That way you're being honest with them.

SKATE PARK

Help this lost unicorn skate her way through the maze to find her friend.

WHICH WAY?

Which path should Gem and Jewel take to reach Crystal Unicorn?

Which path will lead them to ice creams?

Which path will lead them to the rain cloud?

SEEK AND SPOT

Can you spot all the friends in the word grid opposite? When you do, tick them off and add some colour to complete the pictures.

CRYSTAL

LOVEHEART

SPARKLE

STARLIGHT

MOONBEAM

RAINBOW

STARDUST

DAISY

GEM

JEWEL

LILI

FILBERT

HARRIET

SHIMMER

BILL

CHIRPY

FLUTTERSHY

P Y V H Y N N K F B T T M L
P W G S S H A P O W E K U O
N B I L G Y F G F U I P Y V
Y A I T R E B L I F R V J E
D L B Y U C M V C Z R Q S H
I T H G I L R A T S A I M E
T V G E F S B Y E B H M Y A
J Q A W Q H A Z S G N H S R
W E K L K I M Y X T S T V T
O C W S L M H A P R A Z Y V
B N V E X M K U E R N L N R
N U Y H L E F T D B I Z O P
I W R Z Q R T U K I N H X D
A U Z G L U S B I L L O C S
R V U H L T W X Z K A W O Y
F H I F H K R I K J E K F M
S P A R K L E P X Z L Z F Q
J O S J I V X E Y T I G L Q

BORN TO BE DIFFERENT!

Ever wondered what it would be like to be something completely different? What would you be?

IF I WAS A COLOUR I WOULD BE...

IF I WAS AN ANIMAL I WOULD BE A...

IF I WAS A POP STAR I WOULD BE JUST LIKE...

IF I WAS A CHOCOLATE BAR I WOULD BE A...

IF I WAS A MOVIE STAR I WOULD BE JUST LIKE...

IF I COULD LIVE IN AN ONLINE GAME I WOULD LIVE IN...

IF I WAS AN ICE-CREAM FLAVOUR I WOULD TASTE LIKE...

IF I WAS A NUMBER I WOULD BE NUMBER...

IF I COULD BE ANYONE IN THE WORLD I WOULD BE...

IF I WAS A PLANET I WOULD BE...

IF I COULD GIVE MYSELF A NEW NAME IT WOULD BE...

IF I WAS A FLOWER I WOULD BE A...

IF I WAS A SUPERHERO I WOULD BE...

Spot It

The smaller pictures may all look the same as the big picture, but there is something different in each one. Can you spot what?

YUM YUM!

The unicorns are at the ice cream cart. Can you work out what they choose, based on what they like?

Hidden Message

Use this super stealthy way to write secret notes to your BFFs! Just follow the steps below to create some invisible ink.

What you need:

- 1 bowl
- 2 cotton buds
- ¼ cup of baking soda
- ¼ cup of water
- ¼ cup of a dark coloured juice, like cranberry juice
- white paper

What you do:

1. Ask an grown-up to help you add the water and baking soda to a bowl, and carefully mix them together.
2. Dip a cotton bud into the mixture.
3. Use the cotton bud to write your message on the paper.
4. Wait until the ink is completely dry.
5. Dip the other cotton bud into the juice.
6. Paint the juice over your message and wait for it to appear – just like magic!

Ask a grown-up to help with the tricky bits.

ODD ONE OUT

Can you spot the odd unicorn out in each row?

1

2

3

4

5

6

PLAY TIME

Check out these fun games to play with your friends.

GO TEAM UNICORN

INSTRUCTIONS:

- choose one player to go off and hide
- the rest of the players must seek them out
- when they find them, they must sqaush into the hiding place with them
- the last person to find them becomes the hider for the next game

Treasure HUNTERS

INSTRUCTIONS:

- Gather together around 10 items of treasure - these could be anything, for example, coins, biscuits, socks, hair bobbles etc
- ask all the players to close their eyes, while you hide all the treasure items - you could hide them in a room, or around a house or garden
- the players then have five minutes to find all the treasure, the player who finds the most items, wins

WHO AM I?

INSTRUCTIONS:

- fill a bowl with sticky notes with names written on them - these could be names of friends, teachers, sports stars, historical figures or movie actors
- each person takes a note, then sticks it to the forehead of the person next to them, so that everyone has a note on their head and everyone else can read it
- take it in turns to guess who you are by asking your friends a yes or no question
- the player to guess correctly first, wins

MEMORY MUDDLE

Stare at this picture for 30 seconds and try to remember as many things about it as you can. Then turn the page and try to answer the questions.

See how much you can remember about the picture on the previous page and answer the questions below.

1. Who is crossing the bridge?
   - A Crystal Unicorn
   - B Harriet Horse
   - C Filbert Frog

2. How many trees did you spot in the picture?
   - A one
   - B two
   - C three

3. What is growing on the grass?
   - A carrots
   - B gems
   - C flowers

4. Who is splashing about in the stream?
   - A Jewel and Gem Unicorns
   - B Fluttershy and Bill Butterfly
   - C Nobody

5. What is Crystal Unicorn collecting?
   - A sparkly crystals
   - B sparkly stars
   - C sparkly coins

6. Who isn't in the picture?
   - A Loveheart Unicorn
   - B Chirpy Chick
   - C Lili Ladybird

SUPER SELFIES!

Grab your pens and create some selfie pics of you, your friends and the unicorns.

Team UNICORN

Hello cupcake!

BFF!

Create Your Own Unicorn

What colour would it be?

○ yellow heart ○ purple heart ○
○ green heart ○ pink heart ○

What symbol would it have?

rainbow ○ heart ○ cloud ○
ice cream ○ snowflakes ○ shooting star ○

Tick 3 special skills you would give it.

- ○ super speed
- ○ breathe underwater
- ○ night vision
- ○ invisibility
- ○ super strength
- ○ magical horn

Draw your unicorn here.

_______________ _______________

Give your unicorn a name. Its first name could be the season you were born in.

Followed by either the last thing you ate or your favourite colour.

DOTTY FUN

Find a friend and challenge them to this fun game.

1. Take it in turns to draw a vertical or horizontal line between each dot.
2. Each time you complete a box, mark your initials inside it.
3. An empty box is worth 1 point, a gem box is worth 2 points, a heart box is worth 3 points, a rainbow box is worth 4 points and a unicorn box is worth 5 points.
4. When all the dots have been joined up, add up your scores. The player with the most points, wins.

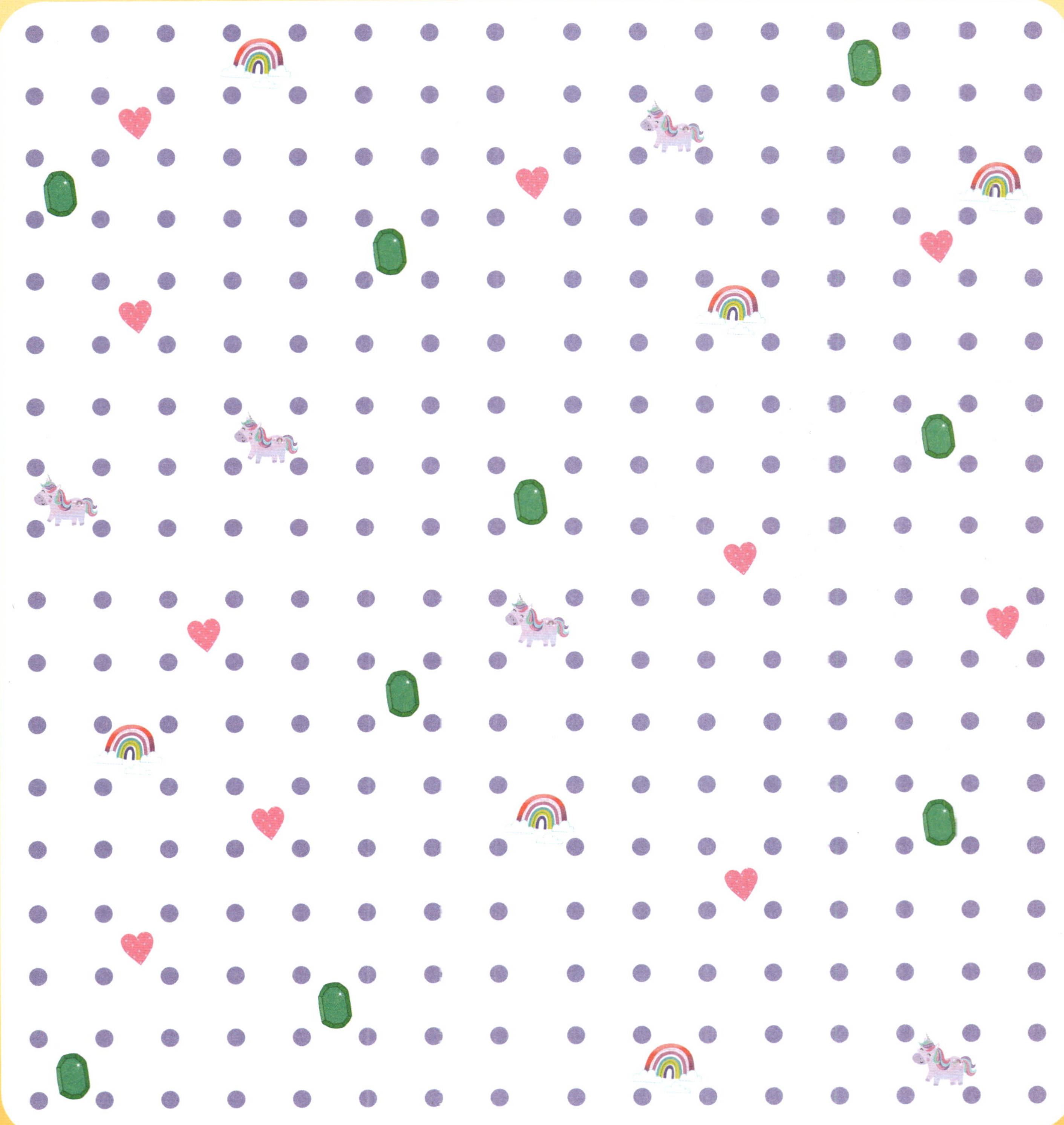

ANSWERS

Pages 6-7

Page 14

Page 8

Pages 16-17

Pages 12 - 13

Page 19